Thomas O´Hagan

In Dreamland

and Other Poems

Thomas O´Hagan

In Dreamland
and Other Poems

ISBN/EAN: 9783744772143

Printed in Europe, USA, Canada, Australia, Japan

Cover: Foto ©ninafisch / pixelio.de

More available books at **www.hansebooks.com**

IN DREAMLAND

AND

OTHER POEMS

BY

THOMAS O'HAGAN.

———

" The world is too much with us. Late and soon,
Getting and spending, we lay waste our powers :
Little we see in Nature that is ours ;
We have given our hearts away a sordid boon !"
— *Wordsworth.*

———

TORONTO:
THE WILLIAMSON BOOK COMPANY, LTD.
1893.

Entered according to Act of Parliament by THE WILLIAMSON BOOK COMPANY, LIMITED, in the Office of the Minister of Agriculture for Canada.

PREFACE.

The generous reception accorded to the first edition of "A Gate of Flowers" has emboldened the author to issue a new and enlarged volume of poems, "In Dreamland," in the hope that the reader will find therein moments of restful pleasure.

T. O'H.

TO MY MOTHER

TO WHOSE

FAITH, DEVOTION, AND LOVE

I owe the inspiration of aught
that is worth recording
in my life,

I DEDICATE THIS VOLUME.

THE AUTHOR.

CONTENTS.

CONTENTS—*Continued.*

In Dreamland.

I DREAMT a dream of the old, old days,
  When life was sweet and strong,
When the breath of morn swept thro' the groves
  Like the notes of a joyous song;
And I knelt beside my mother's knee,
  And lisped in faith her prayer,
When the lilacs bloomed and the roses bled,
  Too full of the morning air.

For the world to me was bright and fair
  In the days of long ago,
When each summit peak was bathed in light
  That streamed to the vale below;
And the birds sang songs in tender notes,
  As sweet as the voice of love,
And the earth was full of roseate dreams
  That ripen'd in faith above.

And I threw my arms about the past,
  Its hopes, its griefs, its love,
As I pressed to my heart each cherish'd thought
  That nestl'd like some fond dove;
And I lived again the joys of youth,
  Made strong through the summer's rays,
As I drank the wine from Memory's cup
  In dreams of the old, old days.

A Gate of Flowers.

O ROSEBUD morn of other years,
  How sweet thy golden light!
Far down the path of manhood's vale
  Thy sun beams warm and bright;
I turn me to that morn of youth,
  And, lingering with the hours,
I feel the breath of childhood's days
  Sweep through this gate of flowers.

And entering in, how strange a sight!
  The flowers are wither'd low,
The Rose that blush'd at eventide
  Is crush'd beneath the foe;
The starry eyes that beam'd with love—
  The lips incarnate red—
Those orphans of the early morn
  Are number'd with the dead.

O sweet-lipped Rose, so dear to me,
  How oft thy pouting smile
Enchain'd my heart with tender love,
  Endear'd me with its wile!

How oft hath memory clad my thoughts
  With hue of purple light,
Caught from the charms that deck'd thy form,
  O Rose of morning light!

How oft I've walked the same old path,
  And pluck'd the floweret wild,
And dreamt a dream of peaceful hope
  That lull'd me as a child!
How often in amber light of morn
  I've peep'd among the trees,
And watch'd the leaves in sportive joy
  Betray the morning breeze!

I love those cheery morns of old,
  Their sunshine bright and clear,
Fair nurslings clad in rainbow light,
  Embalm'd with heav'nly tear;
But, ah! the friends of other days—
  They are the gate of flowers
That bloom with tender memories
  From buds of golden hours.

E'en now I see the blushing Rose—
  Sweet floweret child of grace—
E'en now I see the Lily droop,
  The Fuchsia hide her face;
O tender flowers! O tender years!
  O mornings kindly bright!
Within my heart your memory lives
  In rays of love and light!

The Fever'd South.

A SCOURGE is out upon the land,
　　The breath of Death sweeps on !
　God help the South—the fever'd South —
　　How long, O Lord, how long?
Affliction rests upon its brow,
　　And weak each soothing hand
To stroke the pallid face of Death
　　That looms o'er all the land.

The happy home is rent with wails,
　　And dying one by one,
The mark of sorrow on each face
　　Proclaims a friend has gone.
The stately house and mansion bright,
　　The poor and lowly cot,
Are hush'd in deathlike solitude
　　That wraps the fever'd spot.

O what devoted souls bend o'er
　　The dying on each bed,
And watch the spark of life depart
　　That whispers man is dead !
Yes, truly this must be of God,
　　This fortitude from heaven,
That fills heroic souls with love,—
　　The crowning gift of seven.

Beside a couch of suffering
   A holy Sister stood ;
The cross of hope was held aloft—
   She breathéd words so good,
That Faith beam'd in the dying face,
   While Hope held forth her hands,
And angels wafted o'er the dead—
   God help the fever'd land !

The Old Year and the New.

UPON his couch the Old Year lay,
    Death pressed his brow and hand,
A pilgrim Year in mantle white
    Was dying in the land;
Life's anxious heart stood mourning by,
    And dropt a pitying tear
Upon the cold and snowy shroud
    That wrapt the dear old Year.

O Father Time! O archer swift!
    Thy arrows are but days
Shot through the sky that spans our life,
    Some flecked with golden rays,—
Some clad in raiment dark and drear
    That know no earthly light,
The sunshine of whose joys and hopes
    Are quenched in Sorrow's night.

O happy, jolly, good Old Year!
    We'll miss thy heart and hand;
We knew thy form, we knew thy face,
    Thy smile hath cheered the land.
Within thy folded arms we've dreamt,
    With hopeful prayers and fears,
But now, alas! kind, good Old Year!
    We bury thee with tears!

The friends that gathered round thy knee
  We'll meet, alas ! no more ;
They've left the household of our days,
  And closed the iron door.
Life beams anew—with other light
  We seek our path to find ;
Nor seek in vain, with torch in hand,
  The path we left behind.

Another Year hath robed itself,
  And started on its way ;
With staff of hope and raiment bright
  It ushers in the day.
The bells are ringing through the land,
  All hearts are filled with cheer ;
"The Old is dead !"—"Long live the New !"
  The glad, the bright New Year !

Ring in the joys of happy home,
  The mirth, the love, the glee ;
Ring in sweet peace to all mankind,
  Ring till all hearts are free !
O cherub Year ! O white-robed child !
  Baptized in hope above,
We pray thee bless with heavenly smile
  The hearts and homes we love !

Two Roses.

PLUCKED a rose at eventide,
　　When tears from heaven were falling,
And shadows clad the distant hills
　　That to my heart seemed calling ;—
I plucked a rose, and in its heart
　　I found a dream of childhood,
'Twas fragrant with the dews of youth
　　Still lingering in the wildwood.

Ah, well I knew the dream I found,—
　　'Twas set in manhood's morning,—
A picture of the noonday bright
　　With starry hopes adorning ;
The throbbing heart of early youth,
　　That knew each route and ramble,
Was painted in its glowing cheeks,
　　'Mid bower and brake and bramble.

I plucked a rose—alas, too soon !
　　Its heart was full of sighing,
While health and hope filled every bud,
　　My rose was surely dying ;
The lilac griev'd, the fuchsia wept,
　　Each orphan mourn'd in sorrow,
For dark the night that reign'd above,
　　And dark the coming morrow !

I plucked a rose at early morn,
　When gentle winds were straying,
And balmy air of leafy June
　Through Nature's heart was playing;
Within its folds was wrapt a dream
　Of manhood's gain and glory,
And strength of years and star-crown'd days
　Embalmed in verse and story.

I plucked a rose—alas! so soon
　Its joy-crown'd days were number'd,
Its dream was o'er, its noontide gone,
　In Death's cold arms it slumber'd;
The stars above looked down in grief,
　Earth's blossoms droop'd in sorrow,
The rose of early morn was dead,—
　Its hopes reached not to-morrow.

O rose of morn! O rose of eve!
　O fragrant dream of wildwood!
Within your folds I've slumber'd oft
　In stainless days of childhood;—
Within your folds I've watched the dawn
　Grow strong in noontide splendor,
Then sink behind the hills of blue
　In curtains deep and tender!

November.

HILL-CLAD, cold November,
    Autumn's drooping head,
Weeping skies, psalm like sighs,
    Nature's cold, cold bed.

Dead leaves fall before me—
    Hopes of summer dreams;
Naked boughs, broken vows,
    Mirror'd in bright streams.

Tatter'd robes of glory
    Trampled by the wind;
Faded rays, faded days,
    Floating through the mind.

Days of gloom and sadness,
    Hours of sacred care;
Lonely biers, bitter tears,
    Hearts in silent prayer.

Ireland in 1880.

HEARTS are failing, mothers wailing,
    Hope is drooping o'er the land,
God of mercy ! help dear Erin,
    Stay the famine with Thy hand.
Clouds are gathering, darkly gathering,
    Fast the tide of woe rolls on,
Help dear Erin, oh, ye people !
    Till the wave of want is gone.

"Help us ! help us ! or we perish,"
    Is the cry from o'er the deep,
And the billows of the ocean
    Chant a lonely dirge and weep.
Help dear Erin ! help dear Erin !
    Sounds a tocsin from the dead,
Sounds the voice of armied martyrs
    That a nation's glory led.

They are dying ! they are dying !
    Sighs the breeze upon the stream ;
They are dying ! Erin's children—
    Oh, my God, is this a dream ?
In the midst of wealth and plenty,
    Hunger knocking at the door !
Shrouds of pity, shrouds of mercy,
    Wrap the dead for evermore !

Cold the night and chill the morning,
　Dies the fire upon the hearth,—
Dies the hope of Erin's children,
　Faint each ember quench'd by dearth.
Woe is Erin ! woe her people !
　Famine darkens o'er the land,
Tears of sorrow bathe the nation,
　Suffering Erin—faithful band.

They are dying ! they are dying !
　Sighs the harp across the deep,
They are dying ! Erin's children
　Chant the psalm of death in sleep.
Tears and sorrow—hope to-morrow—
　Beads of woe in silence told,—
God of Erin ! God of mercy !
　Take the dying to Thy fold !

They are dying ! they are dying !
　Oh, affection ! can it be
That the homes of happy childhood
　Sink beneath the woeful sea ?
They are dying ! "*De Profundis !*"
　Lay them gently 'neath the sod ;
"*Miserere !*" faithful Erin,
　Live forever with thy God !

Reverie.

AT eve, as the sun sinks low in the west,
    And its streamlets are kissing each hill,
  'Tis sweet to recline 'neath a bright autumn tree
    That is brooding in silence so still ;

To watch the dark mantle of night fall down
  And wrap the cold shoulders of day,—
O golden hour in the autumn of life,
  Stay, linger with Hope's bright ray!

Stay, linger a while in thy sapphire hues,
  And paint me a vision so bright,
That the past and the future shall blend into one
  Like a day and a star-cheering night.

O paint me those sweet-lipp'd hours long past
  When my heart puls'd free from all care,—
When the bright, bright flowers of a rosy morn
  Were breathing the incense of prayer.

Far back, far back in the morning of life
  Glad memory beckons me on
To a garden of hope bedash'd with dew,
  Where visions of infancy throng.

Ah! yes, I am treading once more the path,—
  See, here are the lilacs in bloom,
And the fancy I wove in a wreath one day
  To cover some nameless tomb.

O vision of Youth! O altar of Truth!
  O golden censer on high!
I would that my soul might float, like thee,
  In fragrant balm to the sky!

Tokens.

YOU ask for a token of love, my friend,—
　　A voice from the tent of my heart;
Ah! well may you ask this gift, my friend,
　　In the morning of life, ere we part.

Who knows where the noonday sun may find
　　The forms that we loved once dear?
For the brightest life hath cold, cold storms,
　　And below each glad joy is a tear.

The mother who sits by her cradle prize
　　Hath token of fondest love;
Yet the angels are weaving its fate, mayhap,—
　　A bright, bright token above.

What blossom so bright in the garden of life
　　That wintry frost may not sear?
What token from heaven so full of hope
　　Not woven with joy and fear?

You ask for a token of love, my friend,—
　　A beam from the fire of my heart;
Ah! well may you ask this gift, my friend,
　　In the morning of life, ere we part.

A Christmas Chant.

RING in the memories of olden days,
  And the joys of bright Christmastide,
    A wreath of song for the hearts that live,
A prayer for the souls who died.
Ring in the love of a mother's heart,
The faith of a father's tear—
These bind the links of sweet Christmastide,
A golden chain for the year.
      O hearts that love,
      Ye feel the cheer;
      The wreath of song
      But hides a tear.

Around the hearth we miss each friend,
Around our joys fond memories blend;
The broken strings—ah, who will place?
Life's tuneful lyre recalls each face:
The old—the young—the loved ones dear—
Bloom in our heart through memory's tear.

Ring in the starry songs of heaven,
The flame lit hours of happy home;
Across the sky, in distant dreamland,
Sweet voices fill the starry dome.

The heart of June is fill'd with throbbings,
Hark to the laughter of sweet May!
Around the fire bright months of roses
Clasp hands and welcome Christmas day.
  O hearts that sing,
  And know not sorrow,
  Ye dream of hopes
  That light to-morrow.

Come, let us welcome at the door
The friends our hearts have known of yore;
Give to our boards good Christmas cheer,
And crown with flowers the closing year;
Sing 'round the merry, merry song,
The wine of life—in deeds prolong.

This morn—O Faith, and Hope, and Love,
The rainbow seal in heaven above,
The stars chant forth a glorious hymn,
The New Born dwells in Bethlehem;
The hills rejoice, the seas proclaim
The glory of a Saviour's name.
  Gloria in Excelsis Deo,
  Rings the heavenly song,
  Gloria in Excelsis Deò,
  Chants the heavenly throng.
  Gloria in Excelsis Deo,
  From the starry sky,
  Gloria in Excelsis Deo,
  Peals the hymn on high.

This morn, O sinless souls of grace,
Kneel at the crib in lowly place ;
Before the altar of the heart
Let incense pure in prayer depart.
O peace on earth ! O peace in heaven !
Sweet flower of peace at Bethlehem given.

     Gloria in Excelsis Deo,
     Sings the Angels' choir,
     Gloria in Excelsis Deo,
     Strikes the heavenly lyre.
     Gloria in Excelsis Deo,
     Hark the notes afar !
     Bonæ voluntatis,
     Bethlehem's heavenly star !

The Funeral Bell.

KNELL ! knell ! knell !
 Rings through the air the funeral bell ;
  Fraught with cold woe,
  Now high, now low—
  Tolling so mournfully,
  Tolling so lornfully,
Deep-toned, grief-toned, sorrowful bell !

  Knell ! knell ! knell !
Peal the sad notes of the funeral bell ;
  Dismally—drearily—
  Ever so wearily,
  Float the sad tones,
  Echo'd in moans,
Down the dark dome of the funeral bell.

  Knell ! knell ! knell !
Ever the same sad story to tell :
  Just a lone bier—
  Memory's tear—
  Shroud them in dust,
  Sinful and just !
Peal the sad notes of the funeral bell.

Knell ! knell ! knell !
Dirges of woe the heart knows so well ;
Tolling on high,
Tolling each sigh—
Anthems of gloom,
Psalms from the tomb,
Deep-toned, grief-toned, sorrowful bell !

Profecturi Salutamus !

A Graduation Poem, read at the Ottawa University Commencement
Exercises, June, 1882.

HAIL, seat of learning ! temple of each art !
    Thy clustering fame salutes us as we part !
    Bright is the morn within thy classic walls,
Pleasant each sweet-lipp'd hour when duty calls ;
Mine be the task—a pilgrim at thy shrine—
To weave in verse the glory that is thine !

This is our golden day, its memories dear
Will bud and bloom with each returning year ;
When winter's frost has chilled the throbbing lyre,
Its chords will ring by life's decaying fire,
And every beam that warms our breast to-day
Will burn a star o'er life's declining way.

Before we part, ere yet the dews of eve
Have dimm'd our sight or taught the heart to grieve,
While rosebud blushes on the cheek of June,
And groves are vocal with their minstrel's tune,
We fain would linger 'round thy altar fires,
And warm our hearts and hands with scholar sires.

Not thus, not thus—the sun is sinking fast,
Its last bright-curtain'd ray, and all is past ;

Our college morn rejoicing in the east,
Each student brings a flower to crown the feast—
The noon is hot, the toil and labor o'er—
See, here we stand, kind parents, at the door.

The race was long, each mile-stone far apart,
Now through the mist of time we see the start ;
Ah ! how the rounded years gleam in our mind,
Fair memories bright'ning as they roll behind ;
See by our side good friends, who watch'd our pace,
And mark'd the smile that beam'd upon each face.

Then let us haste ere yet the breath of eve
Has woo'd the flowers our hands would fondly weave ;
The night will come when hearts will be at rest,
And sable curtains hide each honor'd guest ;
The story half begun will not be told
If pulse grow faint and eye grow dim and old.

Sweet are the hours that nestle in the years
While Youth and Manhood join their hopes and fears,
When young Ambition climbs the eastern hill,
And sunbeams dance upon the neighboring rill,—
In triumph scales each student to the cloud,
Nor deems himself beyond the living crowd.

Perhaps he thinks, as Jacob did of old,
When angels climb'd the heavenward stairs of gold,
The dream is good—'tis pleasant all alone,

Here will I rest upon this cloudy stone ;
To-day we reach a height flush'd with a ray,
Then pour the oil and consecrate the day.

Yes, pour the oil upon each reverend name
That gilds our temple with its clustering fame ;
Long may its sacred counsels guide our heart,
Our Alma Mater, shrine of Truth and Art !
Long may its glories shed bright lustre round
The hallow'd scenes our hearts to-day have crown'd !

And now, kind friends, the fast-declining ray
Fades to the twilight of our golden day ;
With grateful voice we whisper fond farewell !
And wave our hands and toll the curfew bell !
We hail you, greet you, friends and Fathers dear,
Crown'd with bright flowers of love from year to year !

The Maple and Shamrock.

ET'S sing of the Maple, the broad, gen'rous Maple,
  A type of our country, fair, lovely, and free,
And with it entwine in couplets the Shamrock,
  An emblem of union, bright symbol of three;
In joyous orison let each bounding river
  Proclaim, as it rolls its bright waves to the sea,
That liberty, peace, and patriot devotion
  Will flourish where Maple and Shamrock agree.

Hail, then, broad-leaf'd Maple, fair type of our country,
  May Canada's sons grow as stalwart as thee,
And with the same vigor bud forth into manhood,
  Bright forest of greatness, in one mighty tree;
May virtue ennoble each deed of our country,
  In letters of gold be emblazon'd her name,
Towering up like the Maple, yet humble as Shamrock,
  An ægis of safety, a triumph of fame.

Yes, this be the grandeur we seek for our country,
  Let virtues be Nobles and toil be our King,
The axe of the woodman, while smiting the forest,
  In bold proclamation our greatness shall ring;—

Shall echo the accents of Canada's future,
   In pæan of labor, in triumph of song,
And the grace notes of progress that greet our Dominion
   Proclaim that the Maple and Shamrock are one.

Then weave in one garland the Maple and Shamrock,
   A nation's sweet incense breathe fragrance around,
The pulse of our country shall quicken its paces,
   As quicken the measures of freedom's bright sound.
May the dove of true peace wing its way o'er the country,
   Our people grow great in the sunshine of prayer,
And Maple and Shamrock, resplendent in beauty,
   Embalm in sweet incense loved Canada fair !

In Memoriam.

Mary Estella Spoor, died September 28th, 1881.

DEAD—sweet floweret of faith,
  Gone to thy Father above!
Gone like a ray of the morn,
  Beam from the ark of God's love.
Now sorrow keeps watch at the door,
  While we bow to Death's chast'ning rod!
At the altar of Mary we kneel
  And pray for the floweret of God.

Dead—sweet emblem of grace—
  Star in the rosary of Heaven!
Our tears are but rainbows of hope
  Illuming each prayer that is given.
How short was thy sweet, tender life!
  How rich in the perfume of love!
Rest to thy pure bright soul
  With Jesus and Mary above!

Dead—dear child of thy God,
  Yet living in memory here!
For souls that are holy and good
  Live embalm'd in the heart like a tear.

No more from the Convent walks
  Will thy footsteps be heard in the hall,
No more at the altar of prayer
  In response to thy Master's call.

Dead—and we live in to-morrow
  Through hopes and thorns and fears;
Dead—but thou livest forever,
  And we but a few short years!
Dead—while we chant " *De profundis* "
  In cloudlets of sorrow and care!
" *Miserere !* " my God! " *Miserere !* "
  We kneel at Thy altar in prayer!

An Ode to the New Year.

GOD bless our land! with Faith's right hand
　　Shower blessings on our people,
From waste of snow to city bright,
　　Ring love from every steeple;
From hearts where fondest hopes abide,
　　In regal homes of splendor,
Send forth to all, in cot and hall,
　　A message pure and tender!

God bless our land! with patriot hand
　　Inscribe her brightest story,
Across the span of future years,
　　In deeds of deathless glory;
From east to west, from north to south,
　　Shower blessings on our people,
From waste of snow to city bright
　　Ring love from every steeple!

God bless our land! with Faith's right hand
　　Heal bitter Strife's unkindness,—
And wounded hearts win back in love
　　From Passion's rule and blindness;—
God bless our hearts! God bless our homes!
　　Shower blessings on our people!
In purest chime, thro' endless time,
　　From heavenly church and steeple!

In Memoriam.

Very Rev. Dr. Tabaret, O.M.I., President of Ottawa University,
Died Sunday, February 28th, 1886.

HOW vain are words when sorrow strikes,
 And hearts are bowed in tear-clad prayer,
When in the sanctuary of the soul
 We feel the pang grief cannot share !
A *Father*, loving, kind, and true,
 A *Priest* of great and noble part,
A *Friend* whose every word of grace
 Brought sunshine to each troubled heart
Is dead !—and we his orphans mourn
 As ones bereft of tender care,
And kneeling with our face to God
 We bathe our souls in requiem prayer.
No more his gentle voice will lead
 Our steps through walks of kindly light ;
No more with torch of Faith in hand
 He'll guide our minds to heavenly height ;
O mitred Prelate ! Pastor great !
 O Statesman ! strong in honor's way,—
His was the heart of gifted love
 That watch'd your future thro' each day.
O fathers, priests, and friends most dear !
 When lips are sealed we grieve above,—

When bead by bead we tell in prayer,
  Our tears ascend to heaven in love.
God grant our saintly father rest
  His armor of the earth laid by,—
" He fought the fight, he kept the faith,
  We pray his soul may dwell on high !

Memor et Fidelis.

A Poem Commemorative of College Days, read at the Annual Reunion
of the Alumni of Ottawa University, June, 1885.

COMRADES of the old, old days,
   Who touch the chords of other years,
And gather flowers of sweetest May,
   To crown our joys with Memory's tears !
Ye who have known the gladsome toil
   That stirred our hearts with manly strife
Within St. Joseph's classic walls,
   Whose sunbeams cheered our College life,

Look back through vistas of the past,
   ' And view the forms of olden days—
The waves have ebb'd, our thoughts take flight—
   Old hearts are singing boyhood's lays ;
Hear in the halls that classic step
   That tells of Cæsar's march through Gaul,
And how the Greek in Virgil's verse
   Spun out a tale for *Ilium's* fall.

In bold crusade we touch the shore
   Where Sidon leans upon the sea,
And Richard's hosts a banner bore
   To lead their king to victory ;

And now where Grecian valor stood
    ·Beside that narrow strait of heat,
Leonidas with Spartan band
    Falls on his shield in brave defeat.

But hark! from out the belfry tower
    A chiming summons greets each class,
And Roman, Greek, and sons of Gaul
    With baseballs storm the *narrow pass;*
In centre field 'tis Hector's catch,
    With Achilles behind the bat;
"The *pitcher* oft goes to the well,"
    But ne'er is "broken up" for that.

And out upon the velvet green
    The battle rages fierce and long,
The Rugby rules are all the go,
    The ball pitched round like some old song;
Beside the flag great Cæsar falls,
    For Brutus kicked him on the shin,—
The victor runs, the vanquished cries,
    "The goal! the goal! *tu quoque* Quinn!"

But stay, illusion!—Stay, fond theme!
    Are we the boys of long ago?
Has each one plucked a floweret wild
    From Memory's garden—white as snow?
Ah, yes! I read in every eye
    That beams in friendship round this board

1

That pulse of hand and pulse of heart
  Throb from the fire of Memory's chord.

What care we for the ragged verse
  If but the heart speaks in each line?
'Tis not the sunbeams on the grape,
  But friendship's smile, that warms the wine.
Bring me the lyre with tuneful strings,
  For I would sing of College days,
And fling each number from my heart
  Flecked with a star of tender rays.

We *are* the boys, but somewhat changed
  Since first we left our mother's lap,
And her kind words in sweetest tone
  Proclaimed us fledged with gown and cap.
See, yonder is our *Magister*,
  Who rules the board with grace and art;
You think his hair is growing white?
  'Tis but the flowering of his heart.

And look! here's one with brief and gown,
  Who pleads *Supreme* before the Court;
In olden days he joked so much,
  We thought him fit for nought but sport.
And by his side a fair-haired boy,
  Whose tongue and mine could ne'er agree,
Is now a *pillar* of the state,
  A full-fledged, happy, great M.D.

But ah! my comrades, pause a while,
　Our holiest memories are above;
For God has blessed our College home
　With priests our hearts in reverence love.
We count the triumphs won in life
　By dint of toil and worldly care;
Yet who will keep in record bright
　The victories won through silent prayer?

Then let us pledge our comrades dear
　Through dews of May and winter's snow;
The wine of memory tastes more sweet
　When pressed by hearts of long ago.
Fill up each goblet to the brim —
　We oft before have made more noise—
Let three times three resound in cheers,
　Hail, grand old College! Dear old Boys!

Memory's Urn.

A Poem commemorative of College Days, and Dedicated to the Professors
and Students of St. Michael's College, Toronto.

HALLOW'D scene of boyhood's morn,
   When Hope held high her lamp above,
And dreams of manhood flushed the days
   Bright-ringed like sunlit skies of love ;
Through vistas clad with purple toil
   I view the honied hours once more,
And clasp the hand of comrades fond,
   And greet each heart at Memory's door.

Come in, come in, dear boys of old,
   I know each bird, though changed in plume ;
Within my heart – a cage unbarr'd—
   You've nestled long 'mid sun and gloom ;
Within my heart your cherished forms
   Have grac'd the hours of long ago,
When flowers of spring in fragrance bloom'd,
   Nor dreamt of winter's cruel snow.

Across the years that bind my brow
   Fall glints of sunshine from the past,
As sailing swiftly thro' life's sea,
   Morn's crimson streak lights up the mast

The songsters in the grove I hear—
  A tuneful choir of other days,
Whose notes of rapture stir my heart
  Like chords of old mediæval lays.

Ah! morn so bright of long ago,
  When first I sought that classic hall
Where Faith and Science shed their light,
  And duty hearkened to each call;
Where hearts are taught a love of truth,
  Nor filled with anxious gain nor care,
Where toil is but the seal of heaven—
  A psalm of love—a rounded prayer.

O sweet-lipped hours! O golden days!
  That light with joy my darkling noon;
O roses set with petals bright
  That dream in amber light of June!
Fill up my heart with star-clad thought,
  With kindly flames which gleam and burn,
That in the eventide of life
  May glow anew from fragrant urn!

In Memoriam.

The Most Reverend John MacHale, Archbishop of Tuam,
Died November, 1881.

Clarum et venerabile nomen.

DEAD—great prince of the Irish Church,
　　Strong shield of the poor oppressed ;
Through Erin's heart a sword has pierced,
　　And she kneels by her dead in the west.

And the morning breaks, through tears and sighs,
　　O'er the brow of the dear old land ;
But the widow'd mother wails and weeps
　　For Erin's strong right hand.

Dead—with the sacred fruits of years
　　Garner'd in faith above ;
On the altar of God, as tapers bright,
　　Flame deeds of the Prelate's love.

Dead—but the sun of his life shall live—
　　Shall beam through a nation's tear ;
And the crozier-hand and the gifted tongue
　　Shall bless each heart at his bier.

Dead—with a century kneeling by—
　　The snow-crown'd years of the past,
With mitred heads and trembling lips,
　　Utter the prayer "At last !"

Moore Centenary Ode.

A Poem Read at the Moore Centenary Celebration, Belleville, 1879.

I.

HAIL, bard of Erin, Ireland's greatest poet!
    An aureole of fame enshrouds thy name to-night;
The chords of Tara's harp shall vibrate through the
      world,
    And fill each Irish heart with gladness and delight.
Mute hung that harp, its string of sorrow pining,
    Till tun'd by thee to Freedom and to Song,
Its thrilling notes in mournful silence slumber'd,
    And deathlike spoke of Ireland's grief and wrong.

II.

Proudly thy genius grasped each note and number,—
    Each lay of mirth, each sad and plaintive strain
Told of a people dreaming hopes of freedom,
    While clinging to them press'd dark slavery's chain;
And as thy impulse touch'd the lyre of Erin,
    A gleam of hope beamed through a nation's tears,
Which, bright'ning, shone with such resplendent glory
    That, for a season, Hope dispell'd all fears.

III.

Well didst thou sing of Ireland's ancient glory,
   Ere fair-haired Saxon wrought a nation's wrong,
When Brian's harp told that the Danes were vanquish'd,
   And patriots wove their freedom into song.
Well didst thou cheer the Irish heart in sadness,
   Till Mirth forgot the captive chains around,
And Memory, fraught with olden days of valor,
   Gave to bright Hope a tinge of Freedom's sound.

IV.

And e'en apart from Irish scene and story,
   In Eastern tale thy genius found a lay ;
On Cashmere's plains—its beauteous hills and valleys—
   A Lalla Rookh will keep thy natal day—
Will weave a crown of Persia's fragrant roses,
   As thou didst weave for her bright bridal day,
And crown thee first of Ireland's gifted poets—
   A tribute to thy great immortal lay.

V.

A hundred years have passed, and dear old Ireland
   In every land reveres thy cherish'd name,
And Erin's heart beats high and swells with gladness
   To hear her sons speak proudly of thy fame ;
Yea, e'en in this our own loved, fair Dominion,
   Upon the Bay of Quinte's beauteous shore,
We learn to lisp our own Canadian Boat Song,
   And with thee rest at times our weary oar.

VI.

Hail, then, great bard ! fair Canada salutes thee !
  Thy glory is the glory of our race ;
We'll weave a Maple chaplet with the Shamrock,
  To crown thy fame with beauty and with grace ;
For while Erin lifts her harp upon thy birthday,
  And Irish hearts swell proudly at thy name,
We'll ne'er forget the country that begot thee,
  Whose glory is thine own immortal fame !

The Dawning of the Day.

HOPE ! Hope !
    The hour is coming,
      And the dawning of the day
Fast sheds its mellow glory,
As the sun's bright golden ray
Puts to blush the timid sky,
While each star has shut an eye,
And the tide of morn approaches
In its glory from the east.

    Hope ! Hope !
The hour is coming,
And the little star seeks rest,
As a child that, growing weary,
Nestles to its mother's breast ;
All the glories of the night
Lose their soft enchanting light,
For the lord of day approaches
In his chariot from the east.

    Hope ! Hope !
The hour is coming,
And the purpl'd heavens above
Beam upon the dissolution
In Faith and Hope and Love,

As a flash of golden light
Paints with fire each summit height,
And the sky as one great ocean
Fast proclaims the day begun.

Hope ! Hope !
The dewy tear-drops,
Wept in night's dark bitter hour,
Cling like rubies and bright diamonds
To each leaf and bud and flower.
So will sorrow in the breast
Change to rubies and be blest,
And the sun of Hope resplendent
Light the hour.

Another Year.

ANOTHER year passed over—gone,
　　Hope beaming with the New,
　Thus move we on – forever on,
　　The many and the few ;
The many, of our childhood's days,
　　Growing fewer, one by one,
Till death, in duel with each life,
　　Proclaims the last is gone.

Another year—the buried past
　　Lies in its silent grave,
The stream of life flows ever on,
　　As wave leaps into wave ;
Another year—ah ! who can tell
　　What memories it may bring
Of lonely hearts and tearful eye,
　　And hope bereft of wing ?

Another year—the curfew rings,
　　Fast cover up each coal ;
The Old Year dies, the Old Year dies,
　　The bells its requiem toll,—
A pilgrim year has reached its shrine,
　　The air with incense glows,
The spirit of another year
　　Comes forth from long repose.

Another year, with tears and joys,
  To form an arch of love,—
Another year to toil with hope,
  And seek for rest above;
Another year wing'd on its way—
  Eternity the goal;
Another year—peace in its train,
  Peace to each parting soul!

𝕽ipened 𝕱ruit.

I KNOW not what my heart hath lost,
  I cannot strike the chords of old;
The breath that charmēd my morning life
  Hath chilled each leaf within the wold.

The swallows twitter in the sky,
  But bare the nest beneath the eaves;
The fledglings of my care are gone,
  And left me but the rustling leaves.

And yet, I know my life hath strength,
  And firmer hope and sweeter prayer,
For leaves that murmur on the ground
  Have now for me a double care.

I see in them the hope of spring,
  That erst did plan the autumn day;
I see in them each gift of man
  Grow strong in years, then turn to clay.

Not all is lost—the fruit remains
  That ripen'd through the summer's ray;
The nurslings of the nest are gone,
  Yet hear we still their warbling lay.

The glory of the summer sky
   May change to tints of autumn hue;
But faith that sheds its amber light
   Will lend our heaven a tender blue.

O altar of eternal youth!
   O faith ·that beckons from afar!
Give to our lives a blossomed fruit—
   Give to our morns an evening star!

A Dream of Erin.

I DREAMT a dream, 'twas Ireland seen
  In distant years beyond,
Enthron'd and crown'd, a beauteous gem,
  Earth's idol, cherish'd fond,—
And nations pass'd before her,
  And courtiers grac'd her halls,
And the song of Mirth and Freedom
  Prov'd her battlement and walls.

The wounds and scars of olden days
  Had left her maiden brow,
And manly hearts stood by her side,
  And swords spoke of a vow—
That Ireland, dear old Ireland,
  Should forever more be free,
And her patriot sons in union
  Drive the Saxon o'er the sea.

I saw the Shannon pour along,
  In joyous accents clear,
Its tide of music sweet and strong—
  Each wave was filled with cheer ;
And hast'ning on in proud acclaim
  Swept Barrow, Suir, and Lee :
For a nation's heart was throbbing
  In each wavelet to the sea.

O land of woe and sorrow,
    When shall come this vision bright?
When shall beam a glad to-morrow?
    When shall fade thy starless night?
I have watch'd and waited for thee,
    I have hoped for thee in fear,
I have caught thy ray of sunshine
    Through the ocean of a tear!

My Path.

I KNOW not where my feet may tread in future years,
Thro' garden walks of dreamy flowers in fragrant
bloom,
Or down the narrow, thorny way beset with toil,
That winds thro' vales of sacred tears.

I know not if the purple morns will ope for me
Rich gifts of pearls and jewell'd crowns;
My path may be a lonely waste of blighted hopes,
Nor lamp, nor star lend kindly cheer that I may see.

I only know that faith will light my future way;
That, torch in hand, I cannot fear the darkest hour
That 'round my path may spread its gloom,
If Heaven direct my steps thro' endless day.

My Native Land.

Y native land, how dear to me
The sunshine of your glory!
How dear to me your deeds of fame,
Embalm'd in verse and story!
From east to west, from north to south,
In accents pure and tender,
Let's sing in lays of joyous praise
Your happy homes of splendor,
Dear native land!

Across the centuries of the past,
With hearts of fond devotion,
We trace the white sails of your line
Through crest'd wave of ocean;
And every man of every race
Whose heart has shaped your glory
Shall win from us a homage true
In gift of song and story,
My native land!

O let not petty strife e'er mar
The bright dawn of your morning,
Nor bigot word of demagogue
Create untimely warning!

Deep in our hearts let justice reign—
A justice broad and holy—
That knows no creed, nor race, nor tongue,
But our Dominion solely,
     Dear native land!

Dear native land, we are but one
From ocean unto ocean;
"The sun that tints the Maple Leaf"
Smiles with a like devotion
On Stadacona's fortress height,
On Grand Pré's storied valley,
And that famed tide whose peaceful shore
Was rock'd in battle sally,
     My native land!

Here we will plant each virtue rare,
And watch it bud and flourish—
From sunny France and Scotia's hills
Kind dews will feed and nourish;
And Erin's heart of throbbing love,
So warm, so true and tender,
Will cheer our hearths and cheer our homes
With wealth of lyric splendor,
     Dear native land!

Dear native land, on this New Year,
We pray you ne'er may falter,
That patriot sons may feed the flames
That burn upon your altar!

May heaven stoop down upon each home,
And bless in love our people,
And ring through hearts—both rich and poor—
Sweet peace from heav'nly steeple,
　　　My native land!

A Song of Canadian Rivers.

LOW on, noble rivers! flow on! flow on!
  In your beauteous course to the sea;
Sweep on, noble rivers! sweep on! sweep on!
  Bright emblems of true liberty!
Roll noiselessly on a tide of bright song,
  Roll happily, grandly, and free;
Sweep over each plain in silv'ry-tongued strain,
  Sweep down to the deep-sounding sea!

Flow on, noble rivers! flow on! flow on!
  Flow swiftly and smoothly and free;
Chant loudly and grand, the notes of our land—
  Fair Canada's true minstrelsy;
Roll joyously on, sweep proudly along,
  In mirthfullest accents of glee!
Flow on, noble rivers! flow on! flow on!
  Flow down to the deep sounding sea!

Flow on! sweep on! sweep on! flow on!
  In a measureless, mystical key;
Each note that you wake on streamlet and lake
  Will blend with the song of the sea;
Through labyrinth-clad dell, in dreamy-like spell,
  Where slumbers each sentinel tree!
Flow on, noble rivers! flow on! flow on!
  Flow down to the deep-sounding sea!

Grosse Isle.

"Not less than five thousand of the children of Erin, flying from famine and landlord tyranny, and stricken by fever, lie buried in Grosse Isle."

FAR from their own beloved isle
　　Those Irish exiles sleep,
　　And dream not of historic past,
Nor o'er its memories weep ;
Down where the blue St. Lawrence tide
Sweeps onward wave on wave,
They lie—old Ireland's exiled dead,
In cross-crown'd lonely grave.

Sleep on, O hearts of Erin,
From earthly travail free !
Our freighted souls still greet you
Beyond life's troubl'd sea ;
In every Irish heart and home,
Where prayer and love abound,
Is built an altar to your faith—
A cross above each mound.

No more the patriot's words will cheer
Your humble toil and care—
No more your Irish hearts will tell
The beads of evening prayer ;

The mirth that scoff'd at direst want
Lies buried in your grave,
Down where the blue St. Lawrence tide
Sweeps onward wave on wave.

O toilers in the harvest field,
Who gather golden grain !
O pilgrims by the wayside,
Who succor grief and pain !
And ye who know that liberty
Oft wields a shining blade,
Pour forth your souls in requiem prayer
Where Irish hearts are laid !

Far from their own beloved land
Those Irish exiles sleep,
Where dream not faith-crown'd shamrock,
Nor ivies o'er them creep ;
But fragrant breath of maple
Sweeps on with freedom's tide,
And consecrates the lonely isle
Where Irish exiles died !

The Song My Mother Sings.

SWEET unto my heart is the song my mother sings
As eventide is brooding on its dark and noiseless
wings ;

Every note is charged with memory—every memory bright
with rays
Of the golden hours of promise in the lap of childhood's
days ;
The orchard blooms anew and each blossom scents the
way,
And I feel again the breath of eve among the new-mown
hay ;
While through the halls of memory in happy notes there
rings
All the life-joy of the past in the song my mother sings.

I have listened to the dreamy notes of Chopin and of
Liszt,
As they dripp'd and droop'd about my heart and filled my
eyes with mist ;
I have wept strong tears of pathos 'neath the spell of Verdi's
power,
As I heard the tenor voice of grief from out the donjon
tower;

And Gounod's oratorios are full of notes sublime
That stir the heart with rapture thro' the sacred pulse of
    time ;
But all the music of the past, and the wealth that memory
    brings,
Seem as nothing when I listen to the song my mother sings.

It's a song of love and triumph, it's a song of toil and care,
It is filled with chords of pathos, and it's set in notes of
    prayer ;
It is bright with dreams and visions of the days that are to
    be,
And as strong in faith's devotion as the heart-beat of the
    sea ;
It is linked in mystic measure to sweet voices from above,
And is starr'd with ripest blessing thro' a mother's sacred
    love ;

O sweet and strong and tender are the memories that it
    brings,
As I list in joy and rapture to the song my mother sings !

Two Workers.

THE man who plants a seed of corn,
And watches o'er it night and morn,
And prays the heavens for kindly cheer
To nurse its heart with dewy tear,
Is doing work of goodly part
Which gladdens hearth and home and mart,
And gives his name an honored place
Within the compass of his race.

But he who builds for future time
Strong walls of faith and love sublime,
Who domes with prayer his gift of toil
Whom neither fate nor foe can foil,
Is doing work of godly part
Within the kingdom of the heart,
And wins him honor brighter far
Than ray of light from heavenly star!

Ju Lowly Valley.

O forth, my heart, and seek some lowly valley,
　　Beneath a sky of bright and tender hue,
　From which kind stars rain down their mystic
　　　splendor
　　And wake the earth with tears of heavenly dew;
Let not the summit peaks of distant glory
　Shut out the peace that reigns within the plain;
Better the flowers that bloom within the valley
　Than tempting heights lit up with arid gain.

Go forth, my heart, nor dream of each to-morrow
　　That mocks the hopes and sunshine of to-day,
For life hath joys that grow within the present,
　　But ripen not if touch'd by future ray.
In lowly valley, peace broods sweet and holy,
　　Full of the vesper tide of thought and prayer,
Bound by the golden clasps of love and duty—
　　In lowly valley, life is void of care!

Our Own Dear Land.

OUR own dear land of Maple Leaf,
    So full of hope and splendor,
With skies that smile on rivers wide,
    And lend them charms so tender;
From east to west in loud acclaim
    We'll sing your praise and story,
While with a faith and purpose true
    We'll guard your future glory,
            Our own dear land !

Your flag shall ever be our trust,
    Your temple our devotion,
On every lip your pæan be sung
    From ocean unto ocean ;
The star that lights your glorious path
    We'll hail with rapture holy,
And every gift of heart and hand
    Be yours forever solely,
            Our own dear land !

To Laura.

ROSES bind thy future years—
    Gifts of joy devoid of tears;
    Stars rain down in mystic measure
Love and light as thy sweet treasure!

Morn and noon and eventide,
Faith and Hope by thee abide;
Throbbing hours of sacred care
Wrap thy heart in vesper prayer!

𝔅𝔢𝔱𝔥𝔩𝔢𝔥𝔢𝔪.

AR in the East our hearts this morn,
   'Neath roseate skies of faith and love,
Kneel 'round the manger of our Lord,
   Where reigns the King of heaven above.
      Venite Adoremus !

And shepherds watching thro' the night
   Hear greetings from angelic choir:
"*Gloria in excelsis Deo !*"
   Ring the notes of heavenly lyre.
      Venite Adoremus !

We bring the frankincense of prayer--
   The faith of souls set free from sin,
The spices of sweet charity—
   A perfumed gift from heaven to men.
      Venite Adoremus !

At Bethlehem's shrine of Christian hope,—
   An altar bright, with love and light,—
We kneel and bathe our souls in prayer,
   While shines the cross on Calvary's height.
      Venite Adoremus !

June is Coming.

JUNE is not here, and yet I feel
    'Tis softly tripping up the way,
The hours that throb thro' morn and noon
    Have caught the glory of its ray;
I lean my ear to Nature's heart
    And count its pulse of anxious care
That holds communion with a plan,
    Deep set in dreams of toil and prayer.

June is not here, and yet my heart
    Drinks in the freshness of its morns—
The rose that blossoms on its cheek
    With light and love my day adorns;
The fields of heaven are tender blue
    And clad with green is hill and plain,
While from each bud and blossom bright
    There bursts a sweet and glad refrain.

June is not here, and yet my soul
    Is touch'd with Nature's throb divine—
The brook that slips thro' moss and mead
    Is to my heart a gift and sign.
Oh, God, I thank Thee for this love
    That binds my soul in joy and tear,—
That makes my life a hymn of praise
    To Thy great works, when June is here!

A Message to Erin.

WE send thee a message, dear land of our fathers,
    We send thee a message across the blue sea,
    From hearts that grow strong 'neath the pine and
      the maple
We greet thee, *Mavourneen,* dear Erin *Machree :*
From the lowliest cot and the stateliest mansion,
    A blessing we waft to thy fame-storied shore;
In the sunshine of faith and a patriot's devotion,
    We wing our heart's message to each Irish door.

Through the long hours of night and the heat of the
    noontide,
    We pray and we dream and we watch for thy sun,—
We watch for thy glory thro' rifts in the cloudlets,
    To ring out our joy when thy battle is won;
For ours is no love that grows cold thro' to-morrow,
    Ours is no hope to be quench'd in a day,—
We are pledg'd to thy cause should long centuries await us,
    To light thy green banner with Victory's ray.

We have watched the brave deeds of thy patriot children,
    Whose hearts beat so long against Tyranny's chain;
In field and on scaffold, in life and in prison,
    They suffer'd and died for thy glory and gain :
Then, Erin *Mavourneen,* we send thee this blessing,
    A token of love from thy exiles afar;
God grant it may shine from the sky of thy future
    With the halo and splendor of Freedom's bright star!

A Jubilee Ode (Modified by Irish Circumstances).

❧

HEAR, gracious Queen, we're loyal too,
    And full of love and kindly part,
    Our tears have trickled to the ground
When famine reigned in Erin's heart ;
We know the age and watch its plans,
Its deeds of fame, its brilliant glory,—
And love you true—*As England's Queen,*
But not in Erin's tear-clad story.

On every field where valor led
Our swords have leapt, our hearts have panted,
To smite the foe with deadly blow,
To rout the foe with hearts undaunted ;
On Afric's coast, through burning sands,
The Arab flew in wild commotion,
Nor dared to meet the waves so wild
That heaved round Ireland's brave devotion.

Dear, gracious Queen, we're loyal too—
And faithful to the land that bore us—
Through weal and woe, through smiles and tears,
Our hearts have sung an Irish chorus:

Across the years that bind your reign
We catch a glimpse of England's glory,
And love you true—*As England's Queen,*
But not through Erin's tear-clad story.

The arts have flourished in your reign—
What art so dear as Irish freedom?
Than wealth of Ind a little love
Will better cheer our hearts and lead them ;
In every land we build a cairn
With pebbles stained with heart-bled sorrow,
That you, our Queen, we hail to-day—
And hail not Ireland's peace to-morrow!

Dear, gracious Queen, we're loyal too—
But not to power that strikes our kinsmen;
For justice loves a kindly deed
And through the heart she always wins men :
Look to the land of ivied tower—
Of ruined castle, old and hoary,
And say, great Queen of Britain's realm,
Have you a pride in Ireland's story ?

Oh, mighty voices of the past,
Long hushed in death in Ireland's pleading,
O'Connell, Davis, Mitchell, Butt,   ·
Join hearts with those who now are leading !
And tell us what have *fifty years*
Brought to a land 'neath cruel oppression?
From every mound and patriot grave
Come forth one great heav'n-swept procession !

Dear, gracious Queen, we're loyal too—
In cabin, cot, and stately mansion,
And love you true—*As England s Queen—*
Your wealth of power and cash expansion :
But blame us not if in our cot
We mourn because the *crowbar stings us,*
And crying for bread you reach a stone—
The gift each tyrant landlord brings us.

Dear, gracious Queen, we're loyal too—
And faithful to the land that bore us ;
Though darkest hour beset our way
Our hearts will sing an Irish chorus ;
For *tenfold fifty years* have we
Knelt at the shrine of Ireland's glory—
We love you true—*As England's Queen,*
But not through Erin's tear-clad story !

Decoration Day.

❦

WHAT shall we sing of our heroes
    Who died on the field of fame,
Whose patriot deeds of devotion
    Our loving hearts proclaim?
Shall we count the stars of their glory,
    And tell how they fought to save
The flag of our home and country,
    Now floating above each grave?

No; ours is a simple duty,
    Devoid of triumph and tongue,
With meaning far deeper and greater
    Than bard or poet has sung:
Our hearts must time to their measure,
    Our feet keep pace to their tread,
If we would be worthy to honor
    The graves of our deathless dead.

The world is linked with cycles,
    Each lit with the glory of man,
Whose rays of ripen'd splendor
    Stream'd forth when Freedom began:

For Persian yielded to Grecian
    Till Roman valor wón all,
Then the voice of the North rang loud and strong
    That Rome itself must fall.
Where now is the Spartan soldier
    Who fought with spear and shield,
Who lisped the names of the warlike gods,
    That taught him never to yield?
Where now are the Roman legions
    That answered to victory's call,
And smiled when the voice of Cæsar
    Sounded the march to Gaul?

They live in the heart of history,
    But not in the hearts of men,
Their names are red with the crimson stain
    Of conquest's crime and sin ;
They had no message of freedom,
    They knelt at no altar but fame,
The gifts they brought to their vanquished foes
    Were slavery, sin, and shame.

But the years have blossomed with newborn thought,
    Adown long centuries' plain,
And the seed oft sown with Freedom's hand
    Has ripen'd for man—not gain :
For the noblest thought in the world to-day
    Takes counsel with Freedom's plan
To snap in twain the bondsman's chain,
    A bid him stand forth a Man !

Then honor and love and tears we bring
 To each grave of our patriot dead,
To the soldier who hearken'd to duty's voice,
 To the great strong heart that led:
We shower o'er each breast long, long at rest,
 In rainbow blossom and hue,
The flowers of our heart, the flowers of our home,—
 God bless the brave and the true!

Duluth, Minn.

Erin Machree.

~

HOW dear to my heart is the Emerald Isle,
   With its wealth of past glory—its tear and its smile!
   Its sorrow-clad centuries—starry-crown'd slope,
Now dark with grief's cloudlets—now bright'ning with hope;
How oft in my day-dreams I've felt the strange spells
That bind me to Erin—its vales and its dells;
How oft has my heart gone beyond the deep sea,
To greet thee, Mavourneen, dear Erin Machree!

I have lived in thy glory and breath'd thy air,
I have knelt at thy shrines in the incense of prayer,
I have felt the warm pulse of thy patriot heart,
Now joyous at meeting, now grieving to part:
In all thou hast arch'd my young life with thy love,
As bright as the bow of God's promise above;
And wherever thy star may shine forth in the sky,
I pledge thee my faith and my love till I die.

'Tis strange that, though cradl'd 'neath maple and pine,
My soul should thirst strong for thy patriot wine;
In childhood I dreamt of thy ivy-crown'd tower,
And in fancy I've strayed by thy streamlet and bower—
And I've wandered afar from the place of my birth
To the land of my fathers—the fairest on earth—
And with heartfelt devotion I've wished thee as free
As the home of my birthplace, dear Erin Machree!

Oh, land of my fathers, my faith, and my God,
How I long for true freedom to kiss thy green sod!
Then my soul will sing clear as the lark in the sky,
And chant notes of thy glory that never will die;
For from East unto West, in the warmest acclaim,
Will ring in bright numbers thy deeds and thy fame,
And the harp of thy freedom be heard o'er the sea
In the land of the Maple, dear Erin Machree!

In Memoriam.

MY heart is set to Sorrow's chord,
      I feel the grief I cannot speak,
      My lips would fain the burden tell
And voice my soul, however weak.

For me no more the summer glows,
Thro' beams of earthly love and care,
For he within whose life I lived
Now dwells apart in requiem prayer.

Dear Lord, forgive the tear I shed—
The tribute of a human heart;
In faith I lean upon Thy word,
Let me not from Thy trust depart.

Thou takest from the ripening grain
Whatever holds the dews of heaven;
Teach me to live within Thy will
When Thou recall'st what Thou hast given.

He whom I mourn was Thy good gift—
A father loving, kind, and true;
From day to day, from year to year,
In simple faith his virtues grew.

He knew the world in little part,
And heeded not its noisy din ;
If aught of stain his life did mar,
O Lord, make pure the dark of sin.

For seaward now I look and gaze,
Cut off from land by Sorrow's bars,
And thro' the mists that blind my eyes
I fain would pierce beyond the stars !

In Memoriam.

D. A. O'Sullivan, Obiit September 13th, 1892.

KNIGHT of honor, fearless, brave,
    Champion of the truth and light,
Broad of mind and warm of soul,
    Ever battling for the right.

Gifted heart, we mourn thy loss—
    Mourn thy loss in love and tears ;
Feel the want of thy strong hand
    Through the duty-ripening years.

My Idol.

HEARTS oft bow before strange idols,
　　Strength of power and breath of fame,
　　And forgetful of life's morning
Dream of noontide's gilded name;
But the idol that I cherish
Knows no glory e'en in part—
'Tis the simple faith of childhood
Long grown strong within my heart.

In the darkest hour of trial,
When each star has veiled its face,
Turn I fondly to my idol,
Full of heavenly light and grace;—
Then my step grows firm and steady
Down the mystic path of night,
For the simple faith of childhood
Guides me, leads me ever right.